GREAT MARQUES POSTER BOOK

CADILLAC

ANDREW WHYTE

OCTOPUS BOOKS

Contents

First published in 1986 by
Octopus Books Limited,
59 Grosvenor Street,
London W1

ISBN 0 7064 2503 0

Produced by Mandarin Publishers Limited,
22a Westlands Road,
Quarry Bay,
Hong Kong

Printed in Hong Kong

Acknowledgments

Cars provided by Gerard J. De Persio (page 1), Gordon R. Collins (page 3), Lindley Bothwell (page 5), Jerry Ray Nickel (page 7), Garth Carrier (page 9), Lawrence L. Seidell (page 11), Don Reel (page 13), Paul Shinnerer (pages 15 and 25), Owen R. Crain (page 17), Gaines L. Adcock (page 19), William Jahant (page 21), Jack R. Frank (page 23), Alan Ravitch (page 27), Ed Cholakian (pages 29, 31 and 33), Tracy K. Sheffield (page 35), Ted Davidson (page 37), Ed Berry (page 39), Vern Brown (page 41), Emmet Lawrence (page 43), A. Wolfe Motors (page 45), General Motors (page 47)

Page 1 Interior of a 1958 Cadillac Eldorado Biarritz convertible
Page 3 1941 Cadillac convertible sedan

Special photography by John Lamm (pages 7–11, 15–19, 23–25, 35–39, 43, 47) and Dennis Adler (pages 1–5, 13, 21, 27–33, 41). Photograph on page 45 by Nicky Wright

CADILLAC
CALIFORNIA
41 CADDY

Introduction

With remarkable consistency over the course of many years, the Cadillac automobile has come to represent the ultimate in motoring – American style. That very word, "style," has become essential to the world's hard-selling car industry giants. "Styling" was created as a conscious exercise in the 1920s, and the biggest of all corporations, General Motors (of which the Cadillac Division is the prestige arm), was the instigator. The Cadillac and its associated marque LaSalle were GM's style setters.

The Cadillac's reputation as a great marque has held firm, though, and to do this it has had to offer more than just style. Along with Rolls-Royce, the Cadillac represents quality and integrity, and both names have become synonymous with the best.

To understand the vision of excellence established by the Cadillac, however, it is necessary to examine its origins. The name itself derives from the French founder of Detroit, Michigan. The man who chose it, Henry Martyn Leland, did so because he admired pioneers, and because he had no desire for personal glory.

The eighth child of a long-established New England farming family, Leland was born in Vermont in 1843. He was an apprentice when, in 1861, the American Civil War began. Too young to join the Union army, he had a natural engineering talent that became evident in his work on machine design and setting for the makers of Springfield rifles. With the return of peace, Leland became a senior toolmaker for the Colt company, which applied strict quality control and could produce spare parts guaranteed to fit accurately into any weapon for which they were made.

In 1872, Henry Leland joined the firm of Brown & Sharpe of Providence, Rhode Island, for whom he developed and perfected the universal grinder: a machine of great importance to manufacture within fine tolerances. Leland's career blossomed, as did that of his son Wilfred who followed him into industry. Such was his high standing that, when he decided to set up his own business, he was part-sponsored by Brown & Sharpe. Leland put up some money; his chief backer was millionaire Robert Faulconer.

When the Leland & Faulconer engineering and machining company was formed in 1890, the main products were fine-limit bicycle gearing and power units for steam streetcars. Before the turn of the century, however, the Leland & Faulconer company was supplying a brand-new industry – automobile manufacture. The prices were on the high side, but this firm manufactured to exact specification every time. Leland's most celebrated early work in this field was to make and improve the engines of the first true mass-production car, the "Merry Oldsmobile" runabout.

Many companies began with high hopes only to fail, as the car gained gradual acceptance. One firm due to be wound up was the Detroit Automobile Company, formed in 1899. Instead of winding it up, Henry Leland – as consultant – applied his accumulated skills and principles to the creation of a new automobile. In August 1902, the firm became the Cadillac Automobile Company. Now in his 60th year, Henry Leland put Wilfred in charge of the project, and the first Cadillac automobile was completed in October 1902.

When General Motors was taking shape soon afterward, its founder William C. Durant put Cadillac high on his list of potential acquisitions. Only after prolonged negotiation with Wilfred Leland did Durant win his prize in 1909, at a cost of $4.5 million – and then only on condition that the Lelands kept control. The younger Leland was a sound businessman, and he played a major part in holding GM together during its first crisis.

In 1917 Henry and Wilfred Leland left Cadillac and set up on their own again, choosing Lincoln as the company name, and so creating a second quality marque. Ford took over Lincoln in 1922 but Henry Leland, although nearly 80 years old, was to work on many more projects, almost to the time of his death at 89. Wilfred Leland, meantime, had turned his talents to mining.

Many other great men have influenced Cadillac since the Lelands' days, and kept the marque to the fore among world names. The Cadillac Division of General Motors continues to build the flagships of American industry – yet it always looks to the future, with the introduction of smaller, more fuel-efficient vehicles designed to challenge the best products of Europe and Japan.

The fine automobile shown on the previous page, and the others that have been selected specially to illustrate this book, cover more than 80 years of Cadillac history and depict the wealth of creativity that may still be described as the Leland legacy.

1905 Cadillac Model E Coupe

Cadillac Model E Coupe

The first series of Cadillac cars was called, logically, the "Model A." It was not particularly original but it was manufactured with the commendable honesty of its creator Wilfred Leland behind it. Leland had not set out to make automobiles: he was a disciple of precision engineering and this is what he delivered to R. E. Olds, maker of the "Merry Oldsmobile" curved dash runabout, when he sold him single-cylinder internal combustion engines of exceptional economy and reliability.

There is no doubt that Henry Ford influenced the first Cadillac. Ford was working for the Edison Company in Detroit when his services were acquired by the Detroit Automobile Company; he was not happy, though, with the way his new bosses used him. He claimed that he was not allowed to develop his designs, so he took the plunge and went independent in March 1902.

A few months after Ford's departure, Henry Leland became the guiding light when the Detroit Automobile Company was recapitalized and renamed the Cadillac Automobile Company.

Ford and Oldsmobile practice showed clearly in the first Cadillac car which, at $750, seemed expensive – but it was infinitely cheaper than the other luxury models that came on to the market, for they were handbuilt. From the outset, rigorous controls meant that Cadillac cars always were made to the best quality standards.

The Model A Cadillac, announced in late 1902, had a single-cylinder horizontal underfloor engine and a two-speed planetary gearbox. The vehicle was basic: while only intended for short individual journeys, it was capable of high total mileages.

The format was used for a whole series of one-cylinder vehicles, starting with the 99 cu in (1.6-liter) Model A and continuing via Models B, E, F, K, M, S and T. The later ones had a dummy hood, but the engine stayed "below decks." Nearly 14,000 had been built by 1908, the year in which Cadillac's UK importer, F. S. Bennett, arranged an RAC-observed demonstration of the true worth of the marque. Three cars were completely dismantled, the components jumbled up and then reassembled, after which all three were driven around the Brooklands track in Surrey with no difficulties of any sort. This performance was regarded by Leland as the simple application of his principle of parts interchangeability. Meanwhile, other car makers still floundered around trying to achieve a fit.

Most cars worked, even then; Cadillacs worked better. It was after the Brooklands test that Henry Leland came up with Cadillac's most famous slogan: "Standard of the World."

ENGINE		VEHICLE	
Type	Horizontal, underfloor water-cooled,	**Transmission**	Two-speed manual gearbox
No. of cylinders	1	**Driving wheels**	Rear (via chain)
Bore/stroke	5 x 5 in (127 x 127 mm)	**Length**	106 in (2700 mm)
		Wheelbase	76 in (1930 mm)
Displacement	99 cu in (1620 cc)	**Suspension – front**	Rigid, semi-elliptics
Valve operation	Inlet over exhaust	**Suspension – rear**	Rigid, semi-elliptics
Nominal HP	10	**Brakes**	Rear only

NOTES

Single-cylinder Cadillacs were produced from 1903 to 1908. This "Osceola" is one of the world's very first closed cars.

1909 Cadillac Demi-Tonneau

Cadillac Demi-Tonneau

Whereas the Cadillac Model T of 1908 had a single-cylinder engine, Henry Ford's Model T, introduced in that year, had two cylinders. Since 1904, however, Cadillac had taken the decision to advance quickly and miss out the two-cylinder stage; from that year, too, Henry Leland was in control of all aspects of Cadillac policy.

From 1905 to 1908, the expensive four-cylinder Cadillac was made in small quantities, using the model identifications D, H, L and G, the last of these series being fitted with a sliding-gear three-speed transmission (in place of an earlier outmoded design of planetary). After 1908, the four-cylinder Cadillac replaced the single-cylinder models altogether, and the definitive version was called the Thirty. For several years it was among America's best-selling cars and Cadillac prospered. This was all to the good of General Motors, which Cadillac joined in 1909. At $1400, the original Cadillac Thirty provided luxury car specification coupled to superb value. If the price did go up, then so did the specification.

Much the most distinctive feature of the later four-cylinder cars was the use of electric starting, ignition and lighting systems: largely attributable to Charles Franklin Kettering, an inventive genius whose brilliance became exclusive to GM once his Delco (Dayton Engineering Laboratories) organization was under its wing. This "first" was acknowledged in 1913 by the awarding of the Dewar Trophy to Cadillac for a second time. This British accolade usually went to the car engineering feat of the year.

The Cadillac four-cylinder grew in power, and reasonable economy was obtainable once a two-speed rear axle had been designed for it. This provided a high cruising speed, allied to a low rate of engine revolutions.

An even bolder step was taken when Cadillac followed up a Leland recommendation of 1912 – to introduce a V8 engine. The V8 principle had been tried by many manufacturers, including Rolls-Royce in Britain. It was a de Dion-Bouton unit that inspired Cadillac although the French engine was not particularly efficient. The Cadillac V8 worked well, however, and was the first engine of its kind to be offered in volume production. It replaced the four-cylinder unit from its first season, 1915, in which more than 13,000 V8-powered Cadillacs were made. This soon turned into an annual average of 20,000, except in 1921 when everyone took a postwar dive. The engine was improved for 1924 with the introduction of Charles Kettering's two-plane crankshaft. This made the Cadillac V8 the world's smoothest-running car engine at all speeds. From 1924 there was four-wheel braking to match the performance.

ENGINE		VEHICLE	
Type	Vertical, in-line water-cooled	**Transmission**	Three-speed manual gearbox
No. of cylinders	4	**Driving wheels**	Rear (via shaft)
Displacement	226 cu in (3700 cc)	**Length**	150 in (3800 mm)
Valve operation	Side	**Wheelbase**	106 in (2700 mm)
Carburation	One float-feed carburetor	**Suspension – front**	Rigid
BHP	30	**Suspension – rear**	Rigid
		Brakes	Rear only

NOTES

Cadillac 4-cylinder cars were made (with various sizes of engine) from 1905 to 1915, mostly from 1908. Early cars had three-speed planetary transmission, but a three-speed selective sliding gear was substituted in 1907.

1927 LaSalle Sports Phaeton

LaSalle Sports Phaeton

One of the first principles of GM's declared policy was to make models to fill every price gap in the market. From time to time this meant introducing a completely new "companion" marque, as opposed to a model range. Cadillac's companion was called LaSalle and it was introduced during the late 1920s boom.

GM's LaSalle was the first manifestation of "styling" in its purely commercial sense. With General Motors meeting the challenge of the New World's great car-buying spree under the leadership of Alfred P. Sloan, the new marque was aimed squarely between the $2000 Buick and the $3000 Cadillac – and it succeeded.

Cadillac was being run by Lawrence Fisher: a member of the family whose famous car body business was another GM company. If the early Cadillacs had lacked anything, it was a perceived "personality" or "style." Lawrence Fisher was just the man to recognize the desires of the well-heeled playboy; that was what *he* was, when not attending to Cadillac's needs with customary efficiency. When Lawrence Fisher met Harley J. Earl, he found a man who spoke his language.

Harley J. Earl was born in 1893, in California. His father had been a carriage maker there from 1889, and as Hollywood boomed so did J. W. Earl. The coming of the car naturally gave film stars and other personalities a new means of personal expression.

The Earl Automobile Works was sold in 1919 to Don Lee, a major West Coast Cadillac agent. Young Harley Earl, already the king of "customizing," joined Lee and continued to dream up priceless opulence for the stars – at a star price. It was not long before Earl was discovered by Lawrence Fisher and brought to Detroit, where his name soon became a household word.

Earl's first car for GM was the Series 303 LaSalle, launched at a local automobile show in fashionable Boston in March 1927. It had the latest Cadillac 303 cu in (5-liter) V8 engine (hence the designation), and sleek looks unashamedly adapted from France's top prestige car, the Hispano-Suiza. Bright color schemes and a wide selection of body types enabled the customer to possess a truly individual automobile at a reasonable price. Smaller than the regular Cadillac, the 1927 LaSalle was also an outstanding performer. Most LaSalles wore wire wheels, like the example illustrated, which gave them a light touch to go with the subtly curving body lines. Such was the success of his first effort that Earl became an influence throughout GM from June 1927, when Alfred Sloan instituted the remarkable Art and Color Section, thereby introducing styling as a new, and marketable, commodity.

ENGINE	
Type	90° V, in-line, water-cooled
No. of cylinders	8
Bore/stroke	3.15 × 4.9 in (80 × 125 mm)
Displacement	303 cu in (4967 cc)
Valve operation	Side
Compression ratio	5.0:1
Carburation	One updraft carburetor
BHP	75 gross

VEHICLE	
Transmission	Three-speed manual gearbox
Driving wheels	Rear
Length	197 in (5000 mm)
Wheelbase	125 in (3175 mm)
Weight (approx.)	4200 lb (1900 kg)
Steering	Worm & sector
Suspension – front	Rigid, semi-elliptics
Suspension – rear	Rigid, semi-elliptics
Brakes	Drum (four-wheel)

NOTES

First year of LaSalle marque. Also first use of "second-generation" Cadillac V8 engine. Style by Earl; execution by Fisher.

1927 Cadillac Series 314A Convertible

Cadillac Series 314A Convertible

Cadillac consolidated its position at the top of its class during the 1920s. During that decade, production was, effectively, doubled from 20,000 to 40,000 cars a year. LaSalle undoubtedly broadened the Cadillac Division's horizons from 1927, and indeed 1929 saw LaSalle account for 23,000 cars compared to Cadillac's 18,000. This did not suggest any lack of success for Cadillac, simply a vindication of the "companion marque" principle. "Despite its rich heritage and distinguished bearing," ran one LaSalle advertisement, it "costs little more than many an ordinary car." From their 1927 introduction, all LaSalles were V8-powered, and that very fact associated them automatically with Cadillac in the public mind.

The year 1927 was a turning point in the industry. In that year Henry Ford stopped all production of his Model T car-of-the-people, which had provided go-anywhere personal transportation for more than 15 million customers around the world. After nearly two decades the Ford had become outmoded and quirky. Now a fresh start was made with the Model A, and the Ford v. GM battle was about to begin in earnest.

Cadillac, like the rest of GM, was being governed wisely by Alfred Sloan, the man whose uncanny combination of management skills enabled him to shape the corporation as a series of separate organizations that could turn out individual products, yet could be brought together for economic reasons, or to share components and ideas. Cadillac had used V8 engines exclusively since the 1915 model year, thanks to the Leland father-and-son team. They had left Cadillac soon afterward, as had GM's founder William Durant. Under the shrewd Sloan, the image was built upon and by 1924 the Cadillac two-plane crankshaft V8 unit was the sweetest and most powerful engine on general sale.

New engineering blood now abounded, and it was Owen Milton Nacker who took responsibility for the 1927 version of the V8, known as the 314 – representing the engine's swept volume in cubic inches (5.1 liters). Apart from its power, the Cadillac engine demonstrated marvelous torque and flexibility, providing majestic top-gear capabilities. These, coupled with the new consciousness of automobile styling (brought in by Cadillac chief Lawrence Fisher and his protégé, Harley Earl), made 1927 a landmark year.

The Cadillac was given modern and fashionable clothing overnight, and the marque's only weak marketing link was left behind once and for all; and in style the Cadillac, like the LaSalle, bore more than a hint of Hispano-Suiza grandeur. It was certainly a style that paid GM handsome dividends.

ENGINE		VEHICLE	
Type	90° V, in-line, water-cooled	**Transmission**	Three-speed manual gearbox
No. of cylinders	8	**Driving wheels**	rear
Bore/stroke	3.15 × 5.1 in (80 × 130 mm)	**Length**	189 in (4800 mm)
		Wheelbase	122 mm (3100 mm)
Displacement	314 cu in (5150 cc)	**Steering**	Worm & sector
Valve operation	Side	**Suspension – front**	Rigid, semi-elliptics
Carburation	One updraft carburetor	**Suspension – rear**	Rigid, semi-elliptics
		Brakes	Drum (four-wheel)
BHP	85 gross at 2700 rpm		

NOTES

1927 was the last year for the original (though updated) Cadillac V 5.1-liter engine, first introduced in fall 1914 when it developed 70 bhp gross at 2400 rpm.

1929 Cadillac Series 341B Convertible

Cadillac Series 341B Convertible

In 1928 Cadillac introduced another truly significant new feature: synchromesh. The term, like so many other words in neo-Greek jargon, has now become a part of the English language. Chambers's Dictionary records it neatly as "a gear in which the speeds of the driving and the driven members are automatically synchronized before coupling, so as to avoid shock and noise in gear-changing." Just so. The clashless shift made everyone a better driver, and it was a relatively short step to the possibility of eliminating the manual gearchange operation altogether. Cadillac would pass synchromesh on to its junior fellows in GM – Buick, Oldsmobile, Pontiac (formerly Oakland) and, of course, Chevrolet – before very long; in the 1929 model year, however, the feature was shared only with LaSalle. Instead of nickel, chromium plating was one of the season's innovations, safety glass another.

Cadillac had uprated its V8 to 341 cu in (5.6-liter) status for 1928 – actually the marque's best pre-Depression trading year of all. There followed a 341A and, for 1929, a 341B; 1929 also saw an increase from 303 cu in (5 liters) to 328 cu in (5.4 liters) for LaSalle. From 1930 to 1935, Cadillac's V8 was to become even at larger just over 350 cu in (5.8 liters).

Cadillac's great advances in the 1920s are attributable on the one hand to Alfred Sloan's management policies and on the other to the brilliance of Charles F. Kettering, whose Dayton Engineering Laboratories formed the nucleus of all GM research work.

That the Cadillac has survived into the modern automobile age is reason enough to admire these two men and their skilled, dedicated teams. Both were good at selling, and somehow they managed to do this without overselling themselves. Harley Earl did sell himself, as well as his undoubted skills. In later years, Earl's styling excesses would lay Cadillac open to accusations that its superficial glamour might possibly hide technical mediocrity.

No such accusation could be leveled in 1929, when Cadillac and LaSalle were still on the crest of a wave, and Harley Earl's styling had a youthful freshness and inspiration matched only by the work of the traditional body specialists.

In October 1929 came the failure of the New York Stock Exchange. Happily, General Motors held enough trump cards. Its products had a reputation for reliability as well as performance, thanks to the guidelines established by Henry Leland back in the 19th century, before he had founded Cadillac. The V8, astonishingly, would be overshadowed by an even more exotic Cadillac before the effects of the Depression finally began to bite.

ENGINE		VEHICLE	
Type	90° V, in-line, water-cooled	**Transmission**	Three-speed synchromesh gearbox
No. of cylinders	8	**Driving wheels**	Rear
Bore/stroke	3.3 × 4.9 in (84 × 125 mm)	**Length**	215 in (5450 mm)
Displacement	341 cu in (5578 cc)	**Wheelbase**	140 in (3555 mm)
Valve operation	Side	**Weight (approx.)**	4410 lb (2000 kg)
Compression ratio	5.0:1	**Steering**	Worm & sector
Carburation	One updraft carburetor	**Suspension – front**	Rigid
		Suspension – rear	Rigid
BHP	90 gross at 3000 rpm	**Brakes**	Drum

NOTES

1929 was first model year for synchronization of second and third gears.

1930 Cadillac Series 452 Phaeton

Cadillac Series 452 Phaeton

To launch a 16-cylinder car within weeks of the collapse of the New York banks would seem, retrospectively, to be an act of madness. The fact is that Cadillac was already committed to this course in order to maintain its exalted position. Cadillac's luck was that it had an exciting new product with which to woo the wealthy before reins were drawn in tight.

The Cadillac V16, or 452 series, made its mighty entrance at the New York show of January 1930: less than three months after the Wall Street crash, but before the prospects for the immediate economic future of the country had been assessed.

Harley Earl's styling studio influenced the new V16 Cadillac engine, with its two 8-cylinder rows angled narrowly at 45 degrees to one another. The ribbed covers of the overhead valve train gleamed against the shiny black enamel of the blocks, cylinder heads, and exhaust manifolds which surmounted the natural aluminum of the crankcase. Unlike today, the view on opening the hood was an uncluttered delight to the eye.

The 452 cu in (7.4-liter) engine was rated at a conservative 175 hp, and the superb balance built so carefully into the crankshaft design was matched in every other area. Given a sporting body style (like that shown) this Cadillac could touch 100 mph (160 km/h). More often, though, this superb chassis was fitted with formal bodywork for members of the chauffeur-driven classes.

Toward the end of 1930, a shorter (V12) version of the new engine was introduced, but the V16 caught the headlines for it was the only engine of this configuration ever to reach the salesrooms – the only engine that is, but one. The Indianapolis-built Marmon V16 of 1931 was a 488 cu in (8-liter) ohv developing 200 hp. Marmon, however, was in difficulties and only a few V16s were produced, for Cadillac's multicylinder machine had arrived a year earlier and had scooped the pool.

The name "Fleetwood" was (and is) used extensively by Cadillac, for it has the ring of authentic craftsmanship about it. The original company of that name, from Fleetwood, Pennsylvania, had been taken over by Fisher of Detroit, and so was an integral part of General Motors. Fleetwood bodymaking skills found new openings in the exotic Cadillac market.

Over 3000 Cadillac 16-cylinders were made in their first two model years: 1930 (Model 452) and 1931 (452A). Sales of the equivalent 12-cylinder cars (Models 370 and 370A) exceeded 5000. The 8-cylinder cars lost sales in this period but not disastrously. The worst was yet to come.

ENGINE		VEHICLE	
Type	45° V, in-line, water-cooled	**Transmission**	Three-speed synchromesh gearbox
No. of cylinders	16	**Driving wheels**	Rear
Bore/stroke	3 × 4 in (76 × 102 mm)	**Length**	220 in (5600 mm)
Displacement	452 cu in (7406 cc)	**Wheelbase**	148 in (3760 mm)
Valve operation	Overhead	**Weight (approx.)**	4630 lb (2100 kg)
Compression ratio	5.5:1	**Steering**	Worm & sector
Carburation	Two updraft carburetors	**Suspension – front**	Rigid, semi-elliptics
BHP	175 gross at 3400 rpm	**Suspension – rear**	Rigid, semi-elliptics
		Brakes	Drum, mechanical

NOTES

Cadillac's were the only 16-cylinder automotive engines to be produced for any length of time (1930 to 1940).

1931 Cadillac Series 452A "Madame X"

Cadillac Series 452A "Madame X"

Harley Earl strove always to achieve length and lowness of line, but this was just part of the attraction of his early work. It showed a subtlety which, nowadays, seems uncharacteristic of this showman. His 1931 "Madame X" style for Cadillac was a case in point.

Madame X was a name Earl had picked up from a popular play, and it suited his theatrical manner to apply it to a whole series of V16 Cadillac body types. This series showed that Earl was quite capable of applying a delicate touch. The beauty of the Madame X lay in its sharply chiseled and carefully shaped windows, each with a slender bright-metal surround. This was, in a sense, the last of the true aristocrats, for the tendency to round off all corners had begun. The combination of curves and angles emphasized the beautiful "Hispano-Suiza look" which was about to give way to truly "American" styling. The wire-spoke wheels were good looking despite the increasing intrusion of whitewall tires: these pulled the eye away from the fender line sweep that made the car look almost light (it was in fact both heavy and very thirsty).

After achieving good sales in 1930–31, Cadillac would have to hold on to its hat from 1932 to 1935, but Alfred Sloan made sure that General Motors rode out the storm by reducing overheads as much as possible. Cadillac's future was never really in danger, even when production of exotica was reduced to a trickle.

Cadillac's chief rivals – independent Packard and Ford-owned Lincoln – would have to break into the upper-middle price sector: a move that sounded an early warning of ultimate demise for Packard, still one of the most respected of them all. In 1932, the styling of top-model Cadillacs, Lincolns, Packards, and even upstart Chryslers (with their Custom Imperial Eight), would reach a watershed, for the skirted fender and consequent "heavy" look were about to bring to an end a particularly golden age of the American automobile.

Looked at in the context of pricy thoroughbreds such as the Duesenberg, the Marmon, the Pierce-Arrow and the Stutz; or of technical treats like the Doble steamer and the air-cooled Franklin; or of such sheep-in-wolves'-clothing as the front-drive Gardner, Ruxton, and Cord L-29, the first Cadillac V16 and V12 may be seen for what they were: the winners in a rapid endgame. In taking the major share of what little remained of the top prestige car business with these two models, Cadillac assured the disappearance of many other great names of the automobile world – and in doing so, Cadillac thoroughly justified its supreme position in the GM pecking order. Madame X epitomized that special position.

ENGINE		VEHICLE	
Type	45° V, in-line, water-cooled	**Transmission**	Three-speed synchromesh gearbox
No. of cylinders	16	**Driving wheels**	Rear
Bore/stroke	3 × 4 (76 × 102 mm)	**Length**	222 in (5650 mm)
Displacement	452 cu in (7406 cc)	**Wheelbase**	148 in (3760 mm)
Valve operation	Overhead	**Weight (approx.)**	4960 lb (2250 kg)
Compression ratio	5.5:1	**Steering**	Worm & sector
Carburation	Two updraft carburetors	**Suspension – front**	Rigid, semi-elliptics
BHP	175 gross at 3400 rpm	**Suspension – rear**	Rigid, semi-elliptics
		Brakes	Drum, mechanical

NOTES

As with most models illustrated in this book, the "Madame X" Cadillac came in a variety of body types. This Fleetwood sedan carries the number 26.

1931 Cadillac Series 355A Convertible

Cadillac Series 355A Convertible

From the late 1920s, with its acquisition of Vauxhall and Opel, General Motors was closer than ever to Europe; the Cadillac, as a result, probably received as much attention from the leading European body specialists as any other American-made chassis. The master craftsmen of Britain, France, Germany and Italy liked to couple their names to those of important makes; so did the affluent customer, of whom a remarkable number still existed in the early 1930s.

As an illustration of the Cadillac clothed "out-of-house," this automobile stunningly exemplifies the work of one of Germany's most celebrated prewar specialists, applied to the 1931 V8 355A chassis.

Founded in 1864, Heinrich Gläser GmbH made its first car bodywork in 1902, on one of the original Mercedes chassis constructed by Daimler. Subsequently, the Gläser firm specialized in open cars, particularly cabriolets (convertible coupes) of outstanding detail construction, patenting a number of design features. In the early 1930s, it undertook a great deal of work for the new Auto Union (including Audi, Horch and Wanderer).

Gläser built numerous bodies on German Ford and Opel chassis, and had a close association with General Motors' import company. Buick and Cadillac chassis were, therefore, fairly regular recipients of the Gläser treatment. The example shown here is not singular in suggesting that there was considerable American influence in Germany at the time. There is a tendency to think that art and the automobile came together exclusively in Europe, but the same has often happened in the United States.

In Britain the GM importer, Lendrum & Hartman of Albemarle Street, London, was offering a chassis of this kind (the 1931 V8 Cadillac 355A) for £785 or a complete car for £1250. Even assuming that the fitting of a special body would double the price of the chassis, a smart, reliable, and prestigious American Cadillac with British bodywork could be bought for around £1500. In 1931 many all-British products of less advanced or exciting specification could cost much more than that.

It is true to say that in the first three decades of the 20th century the American quality car, as typified by the Cadillac, enjoyed steady sales in Europe. The old Henry Leland dictum concerning parts interchangeability and product dependability was still more applicable to the products of the United States than elsewhere, even in the early 1930s. Only later did their size and the stigma of "buying foreign" restrict the market for North American cars in Britain.

ENGINE		**VEHICLE**	
Type	90° V, in-line, water-cooled	**Transmission**	Three-speed syncromesh gearbox
No. of cylinders	8	**Driving wheels**	Rear
Bore/stroke	3.4 × 4.9 in (86 × 125 mm)	**Length**	217 in (5500 mm)
		Wheelbase	140 in (3555 mm)
Displacement	355 cu in (5786 cc)	**Weight (approx.)**	4190 lb (1900 kg)
Valve operation	Side	**Steering**	Worm & sector
Compression ratio	5.0:1	**Suspension – front**	Rigid, semi-elliptics
Carburation	One updraft carburetor	**Suspension – rear**	Rigid, semi-elliptics
		Brakes	Drum, mechanical
BHP	95 gross at 3200 rpm		

NOTES

This custom-built Victoria was made in Germany.

1933 Cadillac Series 452C Convertible

Cadillac Series 452C Convertible

The Chicago World's Fair of 1933 heralded two new styles of automobile. In a last-ditch effort to survive, Pierce-Arrow showed its Silver Arrow V12 streamliner. This envelope shape was ugly, although ahead of its time.

It was Cadillac's dramatic 1933 Chicago offering that brought the Harley Earl GM styling workshop yet another accolade for restrained good taste. The fastback coupe body, the reversed-bullet headlights, the rounded windows and fenders and the discreet front and rear window dividers made this lovely car on the V16 chassis a practical production model for 1934 – something the Pierce-Arrow showcar patently was not.

An interesting identifying feature of this car, and of the 1933 Cadillac range, was the radiator grille. Gone was the patrician, vertical, "Hispano-Suiza" shape of 1932. Aside from a hint of Ford-Lincoln in its grille design, the 1933 World's Fair Cadillac was truly original and a delightful transition model. Its V16 engine ensured that it would go down in history as a true masterpiece.

For 1934, there came the news that ex-Rolls-Royce man Maurice Olley had done wonders for the Cadillac chassis. Like other GM cars it was given independent front suspension, and a host of improvements. In 1934, too, Nicholas Dreystadt took over from Lawrence Fisher and became Cadillac's operations chief.

As post-Depression business began to regain momentum, more new ideas flooded in. They had to. Harley Earl's "think-tank" had to work just as hard to produce a salable item as engineering chief Ernest Seaholm and his technical staff. All GM departments operated on the principle that they were there to produce profits. LaSalle was not forgotten in all this.

LaSalle had moved closer to the V8 Cadillacs during the worst years. For 1934 a new image was created for it. This companion marque had always had Cadillac's V8 engine design. Now it was given an Oldsmobile straight-8 to keep the price down, and new Harley Earl styling to keep appearances up. A tall, narrow, elegant grille surmounted slim twin-tubular bumper bars, and was flanked by streamlined fenders and "bullet" headlights. Only the five portholes along each side spoiled a nicely balanced effect.

In the meantime, production of the ohv V16 was drawing to a close. It had started well, with 3250 produced in 1930 and 1931; but 1932's tally of 300 was cut by more than half in 1933. During the 1934 to 1937 seasons production averaged no more than one a week. This ohv series was a classic among Cadillacs and its presence in the catalog kept the image alive in hard times.

ENGINE		VEHICLE	
Type	45° V, in-line, water-cooled	**Transmission**	Three-speed syncromesh gearbox
No. of cylinders	16	**Driving wheels**	Rear
Bore/stroke	3 × 4 in (76 × 102 mm)	**Length**	224 in (5700 mm)
Displacement	452 cu in (7406 cc)	**Wheelbase**	148 in (3760 mm)
Valve operation	Overhead	**Weight (approx.)**	4850 lb (2200 kg)
Compression ratio	5.5:1	**Steering**	Worm & sector
Carburation	Two updraft carburettors	**Suspension – front**	Rigid, semi-elliptics
BHP	175 gross at 3400 rpm	**Suspension – rear**	Rigid, semi-elliptics
		Brakes	Drum, mechanical

NOTES

Custom-built Victoria coachwork by Fleetwood was for Robert Montgomery.

1935 Cadillac Series 370D Town Car

Cadillac Series 370D Town Car

Cadillac's 370 (V12) series appeared in September 1930, some eight months after the sensational 452 (V16) from which it was derived. During the late 1920s, word had gone around the industry that Cadillac was going to introduce a V12. Packard had produced its first V12 back in 1915 – only just after Cadillac's first V8 – but discontinued the type in 1923, continuing to add to its good name through straight-8s. Lincoln, Packard, Pierce-Arrow (then under the financial control of Studebaker) and others responded, but not quickly enough. One of the quickest off the mark was the Franklin company of Syracuse, New York, which offered a supercharged V12 of characteristic air-cooled type once its immediate financial problems were overcome: but it was another case of "too little, too late." (And too expensive.)

Cadillac bamboozled them all. Owen Milton Nacker was the man Lawrence Fisher had brought in in the 1920s to keep the Division's engine design ahead of the opposition, and who had helped keep the rumors flying by referring to 12 cylinders when placing outside contracts. If the announcement of a Cadillac V16 at the beginning of 1930 winded the opposition, the subsequent throwaway line – "You'd like a twelve, too? Well, here you are" – knocked it out.

During 1932, the combined output of Cadillac V12 and V16 models within two years passed the 10,000 mark before the Depression killed the market. It had been a small cake but Cadillac had devoured it before anyone else could get a reasonable slice. V12s outnumbered V16s by about two to one at this time. Solid backing from the V8 Cadillacs and LaSalles would keep the Division in profitable business, and therefore able to cope with its worst year of all – 1933 – when its output fell below 6000 units. No worse figures had ever been seen for Cadillac since it had joined General Motors in 1909 – nor have they been seen since. The Depression affected everyone in the business, however, and Cadillac's situation was better than some.

The narrow-angle Cadillac V12 engine was current only for the seasons 1930 (late) to 1937. Total production amounted to just short of 11,000. For 1936 and 1937, the 370 designation was dropped in favor of 80 and 85, as part of an across-the-range policy on nomenclature.

The car shown is a 370D with the seven-seater Fleetwood formal bodywork – one of only 377 V12 Cadillacs built as 1935 models.

ENGINE

Type	45° V, in-line, water-cooled
No. of cylinders	12
Bore/stroke	3.15 × 4 in) (80 × 102 mm)
Displacement	370 cu in (6030 cc)
Valve operation	Overhead
Compression ratio	5.5:1
Carburation	Two updraft carburetors
BHP	135 gross at 3400 rpm

VEHICLE

Transmission	Three-speed syncromesh gearbox
Driving wheels	Rear
Length	220 in (5600 mm)
Wheelbase	143 in (3630 mm)
Weight (approx.)	4410 lb (2000 kg)
Steering	Worm & sector
Suspension – front	Rigid, semi-elliptics
Suspension – rear	Rigid, semi-elliptics
Brakes	Drum, mechanical

NOTES

Brakes were vacuum-servo-assisted. (Cadillac was about to start a switch to hydraulic operation.) Seven-passenger bodywork by Fleetwood.

1940 LaSalle 52 Special Coupe

LaSalle 52 Special Coupe

Following its downmarket plunge in 1934, LaSalle lost its way in GM's formalized patterns for car ownership. It had the style but not the guts: it had originally made its name as a nimbler, neater version of the Cadillac. Things did not look too good for Cadillac's companion. The 1935 LaSalle made news with its "turret top," GM's term for the effect created by modern pressed-steel production techniques soon adopted across the range by the Fisher body division.

General Motors under Alfred Sloan thrived because it reacted quickly to prevailing conditions. And prevailing conditions showed that after three seasons (1934 to 1936) the side-valve straight-8 LaSalle was not regaining its market share at the rate of its rivals. Lincoln's "upmarket Ford," the V12 Zephyr, was an attractive proposition, as were others in the class (such as the "cheap" Packard). GM had to act – it reverted to V8 power in the form of a new 325 cu in (5.3-liter) unit for LaSalle.

Production of LaSalle cars in 1937 – a good year for the industry in any case – shot up to 32,000. From 1938 through 1940, the annual average settled at the 20,000 cars a year level. That, in itself, was not enough. Although once again LaSalle owners could, in the words of the advertisement, "ride behind a Cadillac engine for only $1240," there were not enough of them. There was an in-house price overlap with Buick, and the gap to the Cadillac was too small. For LaSalle as a marque 1940 was to be the last year. The 1940 LaSalle range included the 130 bhp long-wheelbase 52 series – beautiful, but almost pure Cadillac except in its frontal aspect.

There have been many attempts within General Motors to revive LaSalle. First there was a 1941 model, but it was shelved. Then came an end to car production during the war. Harley Earl created the "Motorama" as a spectacular display of GM ideas, and at his 1955 show there were two "LaSalles" of dire dimensions and laughable lines. These cars vanished, although one of them did have elements of the Cadillac Eldorado Brougham to come.

Another "LaSalle" prototype turned into the Buick Riviera of 1963. There would be other possibilities, as recently as the Seville era. Clearly, the name LaSalle still means a great deal at GM.

The 50 and 52 of 1940 were, truly, the last LaSalles. They offered style and value, just as the originals had done back in 1927, when they had provided master dream maker Harley Earl with his springboard to stardom. In its 14 seasons, LaSalle had been a good companion to Cadillac. It seems a shame that it had to go, but its departure did serve to reemphasize Cadillac's position – at the top.

ENGINE		VEHICLE	
Type	90° V, in-line, water-cooled	**Transmission**	Three-speed synchromesh gearbox
No. of cylinders	8	**Driving wheels**	Rear
Bore/stroke	3.4 × 4.5 (86 × 114 mm)	**Length**	205 in (5200 mm)
Displacement	325 cu in (5277 cc)	**Wheelbase**	123 in (3125 mm)
Valve operation	Side	**Weight (approx.)**	3810 lb (1730 kg)
Compression ratio	6.25:1	**Final drive**	Hypoid bevel
Carburation	Two downdraft carburetors	**Suspension – front**	Independent
BHP	130 gross at 3400 rpm	**Suspension – rear**	Rigid
		Brakes	Drum

NOTES

Last full season for LaSalle as Cadillac's companion marque.

1941 Cadillac Series 60 Special Sedan

Cadillac Series 60 Special Sedan

William Mitchell, aged 22, caught the eye of Harley Earl in 1934, through his work as an advertising agency artist. It could be that Earl had seen Mitchell's fine action drawings of the Collier brothers, Barron, Sam and Miles, and their friends racing sports cars on improvised New York and New England tracks. This small group became the self-styled "Automobile Racing Club of America." (The club was re-formed in the late 1940s as the Sports Car Club of America.) The son of a Pennsylvania Buick dealer, William Mitchell remained a true enthusiast for motor sports throughout his career; he also became as legendary, in his own way, as Harley Earl, whom he later succeeded as head of GM styling.

Earl was setting off into his fantasy world by now, starting with the Y-job of 1937, a large open two-seater with hidden headlights and no running boards. Based on a Buick, it had hefty bumpers and a rear deck of exaggerated length, as if in warning of what would come in his postwar GM dream machines. By comparison with the Gordon Buehrig-styled Cord 810, the Y-job was a clumsy effort from the master of GM arts. Earl's protégé was, meantime, making sure that *his* first contribution to GM history would be a Cadillac worthy of the name.

Mitchell's exciting 1938 Cadillac 60 Special wafted a breath of fresh air across the somewhat heavy, hothouse atmosphere of Camp Cadillac. Like the Cord 810 (and the even earlier Ruxton) it dispensed with running boards altogether. Its roof, window, and fender lines were markedly flatter than those of its stablemates, giving it an elegance that more than justified the use of the term "Special" – for it was an extra special automobile. Needless to say, the GM annual model change rule applied; but for four seasons the car retained its original lines. Relatively little was changed for 1939 and 1940. For 1941, however, the 60 Special was given the mouth organ grille treatment (a Mitchell trademark later on) and its front fenders were extended rearward into the door; rear fenders were fully spatted, but this was an across-the-range policy. Many years were to pass before Cadillac rear wheels emerged unfettered into the bright highway sunlight again.

Fully automatic transmission had been in the offing for a long time; in fact Oldsmobile had been offering the GM Hydra-matic Drive as an option since 1939–40 model year. For once, perhaps through caution, Cadillac forwent this particular "first," but it did offer the system for 1941, still very early in the game. Easing the driver's lot was another bright yet basic move designed to keep GM products way out ahead of the competition.

ENGINE		VEHICLE	
Type	90° V, in-line, water-cooled	**Transmission**	Three-speed manual, synchromesh gearbox
No. of cylinders	8	**Driving wheels**	Rear
Bore/stroke	3.5 × 4.5 in (89 × 114 mm)	**Length**	213 in (5400 mm)
Displacement	346 cu in (5676 cc)	**Wheelbase**	126 in (3200 mm)
Valve operation	Side	**Weight (approx.)**	4210 lb (1910 kg)
Compression ratio	7.0:1	**Final drive**	Hypoid bevel
Carburation	One downdraft carburetor	**Suspension – front**	Independent
BHP	150 gross at 3400 rpm	**Suspension – rear**	Rigid
		Brakes	Drum

NOTES

1941 was the fourth and final season for this composite-bodied model; Hydra-matic was offered for the first time.

1942 Cadillac Series 75 Formal Sedan

Cadillac Series 75 Formal Sedan

From 1938 there was no Cadillac V12 engine. The original V16 had also gone by then: it had been replaced by a side-valve wide-angle (135 degree) 16-cylinder unit conceived by engineering chief Ernest Seaholm. The new engine was simpler, lighter and more powerful than the ohv unit and it was fitted to more than 500 examples of the 1938–40 Cadillac 90 series. President Roosevelt had two of them.

The latest V8, still a side-valve, was powerful, so demand for the V16 spiraled downward. From 1941 Cadillac was again offering only a V8: but it produced 150 hp from 346 cu in (5.7 liters).

In 1941 and 1942 the North American car industry was still making civilian products, and in those two seasons the top model was the Fleetwood 75, which came in eight versions, the most costly being a seven-seater Formal Sedan at over $4000. The cheapest owner-driver Cadillacs were priced well below $2000. There was still a 60 Special in 1942 but it had lost the taut lines of the 1938–41 car and had become just another Cadillac. The Mitchell theme was evident in the way the front fenders swept back into the doors, only to sweep forward again.

There was little time to test reaction for sales of 1942 models had only just got under way when, early in December 1941, Japanese devastation of Pearl Harbor brought the United States into World War 2. Before automobile production ceased, Cadillac had taken advantage of the good sales opportunities of 1941 to produce a new record number of cars – over 66,000.

A feature that was disappearing rapidly at this time was the fender-mounted spare wheel: bodywork was growing ever wider and merging with the fender itself. However, even in the early 1940s, there was still space for such a fitment; the placing, though, usually looked very awkward.

The name Fleetwood 75 was to be used consistently for the biggest of the formal limousine Cadillacs right through to the 1980s, and its indiscriminate use has made it rather meaningless. "Body by Fisher" might be a fairer reminder of the great achievements of an organization constantly having to retool for several different ranges, all under the GM banner. The increasing tendency to share body pressings between the marques was only natural, making individual grille treatment and interior design all the more important – to Cadillac especially.

There was, however, never anything else quite like the biggest Cadillacs. In the days when most American cars were really big, the largest Cadillacs still stood out a mile – as was the intention.

ENGINE		VEHICLE	
Type	90° V, in-line water-cooled	**Transmission**	Three-speed manual, synchromesh gearbox
No. of cylinders	8	**Driving wheels**	Rear
Bore/stroke	3.5 × 4.5 in (89 × 114 mm)	**Length**	220 in (5600 mm)
Displacement	346 cu in (5676 cc)	**Wheelbase**	136 in (3450 mm)
Valve operation	Side	**Weight (approx.)**	4910 lb (2230 kg)
Compression ratio	7.0:1	**Final drive**	Hypoid bevel
Carburation	One downdraft carburetor	**Suspension – front**	Independent
BHP	150 gross at 3400 rpm	**Suspension – rear**	Rigid
		Brakes	Drum

NOTES

Hydra-matic automatic transmission now available.

1947 Cadillac Series 62 Club Coupe

Cadillac Series 62 Club Coupe

Not many manufacturers came out with new models immediately after World War 2, and even in the United States there were severe shortages of steel and other basic materials. A few cars were made in 1945, but 1946–47 was the first full model year. Many names had been lost by now: not by design (like LaSalle) but of necessity. The industry closed ranks.

There were only 16 major marques left in North America by 1945, and 12 of them belonged to the "Big Three." GM made Buick, Cadillac, Chevrolet, Oldsmobile and Pontiac; Ford had preserved the famous Lincoln name and the younger Mercury; Chrysler, De Soto, Dodge and Plymouth were still there, too. The others would merge before very long: Hudson with Nash to form American Motors and Packard with Studebaker.

However, 1945 did produce one new combine: Kaiser-Frazer. For a while, Kaiser-Frazer cars were built in considerable numbers. On three occasions, combined production was high enough to put them into the top 12 US manufacturers, but with sad inevitability the company went to the wall after a few years. Before that, the Big Three had already produced more than 80 percent of North America's 3.5 million 1947 cars. The share looked like this: General Motors 40 percent; Ford and Chrysler groups 21 percent each; Kaiser-Frazer 4 percent; Studebaker $3\frac{1}{2}$ percent; Nash and Hudson 3 percent each (with Nash on the "plus" side); and Packard $1\frac{1}{2}$ percent. Packard was still a threat to Cadillac numerically, but it had opted out of the supercar class generally – whereas GM was more than ever determined to keep every Cadillac in the top drawer, and increase production as affluence returned.

The essentially prewar looks – and the side-valve 346 cu in (5.7-liter) V8 – were retained through to 1947, when the best looker of the Cadillac range was the two-door club coupe or sedanet. Its fastback styling went well with the 1942–47 bulbousness. That bulbousness would vanish for 1948, and the Cadillac coupe for that year, with its long sleek tail and curving windshield, was surely to be the inspiration for the Bentley Continental four years later.

Alfred Sloan, although over 70, was still very much the central figure at General Motors in the early postwar days, outliving such former chief associates as Nicholas Dreystadt, William S. Knudsen, and Charles F. Kettering. Harley Earl, on the other hand, was not yet 60 years old, so there was still plenty of time for new flights of fancy. The era of the tailfin was about to begin. Earl did not commit his worst excesses right away. In fact the 1948 Cadillac range would be an outstanding one.

ENGINE		VEHICLE	
Type	90° V, in-line, water-cooled	**Transmission**	Manual or Hydra-matic gearbox
No. of cylinders	8	**Driving wheels**	Rear
Bore/stroke	3.5 × 4.5 in (89 × 114 mm)	**Length**	215 in (5450 mm)
		Wheelbase	129 in (3280 mm)
Displacement	346 cu in (5676 cc)	**Weight (approx.)**	4000 lb (1820 kg)
Valve operation	Side	**Final drive**	Hypoid bevel
Compression ratio	7.0:1	**Suspension – front**	Independent
Carburation	One downdraft carburetor	**Suspension – rear**	Rigid
		Brakes	Drum
BHP	150 gross at 3400 rpm		

NOTES

Final season of pre-tailfin styling. This body type also described as "sedanet."

1948 Cadillac Series 60 Special Sedan

Cadillac Series 60 Special Sedan

For styling 1948 was a good year. There had been many aviatory allusions in past Cadillacs, but none as specific as this year's inspiration: the Lockheed P-38 twin-boom fighter plane. It manifested itself in the tailfins that sprouted fairly unobtrusively in the new 1948 Cadillacs. You had to hand it to Harley Earl sometimes: this was one of those times. The public fell for the year's long, low "Futuramic" shape – a shape that would continue with only detail changes (usually for the worse) until 1953. A sad loss after 1949 would be that of the fastback coupe or sedanet style, its place filled by a two-door pillarless notchback known as the Coupe de Ville.

The 60 Special was again the top-line "personal" Cadillac in the immediate postwar years and would remain so until 1956. It did not have an exclusive shape, as it had done between 1938 and 1941, but it was the style leader just the same. In 1948, the year of the tailfin, it sprouted an emphatic molding on the leading edge of the rear fender. By 1950, the effect would be featured across the range (even on the big Fleetwood 75) as a dummy air intake. Jetplane themes were all the rage.

It was the tailfin which, more than anything, pushed Cadillac's prestige to new heights. Demand rocketed, too, and production soon passed the record (1937) level; 1950 would see more than 100,000 Cadillacs registered for the first time. Another aspect of "Futuramic" styling was the gentle curve of the windshield: divided for 1948 and 1949, but in one pane by 1950. Cadillac led and the others followed; those fins made quite sure you knew a Caddy from behind. The theme was picked up by other GM marques, Chevrolet going over the top with the Impala. Chrysler and AMC (Hudson-Nash) were among the followers. Ford's workaday 1957 Fairlane was to join in.

North America led the world in production techniques to meet insatiable consumer demand. By the end of 1948, more than 100 million automobiles had been built in the United States. The relative exclusivity of the Cadillac is illustrated by its share of the market thus far: little more than 1 percent. Annual sales were to escalate to 2 percent in the 1950s; 3 and 4 percent in the 1970s and 1980s. More and more people wanted to own one, not for any technical or practical reason but because Harley Earl, Bill Mitchell and their teams carried out Sloan's requirements so diligently: woo the customer, then come out with new ideas that bring him or her hurrying back for more. Planned obsolescence was the key to success, and GM's particular skill was in being seen to react to public demand rather than create it.

ENGINE	
Type	90° V, in-line, water-cooled
No. of cylinders	8
Bore/stroke	3.5 × 4.5 in (89 × 114 mm)
Displacement	346 cu in (5676 cc)
Valve operation	Side
Compression ratio	7.0:1
Carburation	One downdraft carburetor
BHP	150 gross at 3400 rpm

VEHICLE	
Transmission	Manual or Hydra-matic gearbox
Driving wheels	Rear
Length	217 in (5500 mm)
Wheelbase	133 in (3380 mm)
Weight (approx.)	4365 lb (1980 kg)
Final drive	Hypoid bevel
Suspension – front	Independent
Suspension – rear	Rigid
Brakes	Drum

NOTES

1948 was the first year to feature Cadillac's unique and now-legendary tailfins.

1952 Cadillac Series 60 Special Sedan

Cadillac Series 60 Special Sedan

It might seem that engineering was totally overshadowed by styling at Cadillac but, quite often, this was far from the case.

The new-style 1948 had had the prewar 346 cu in (5.7-liter) engine producing 150 bhp at 3400 rpm. A well-kept secret, the new 1949 engine had been developed during and since the war. The only major late change was an increase from 309 to 331 cu in (5 to 5.4 liters), simply to be one up on Oldsmobile whose 304 cu in (approx. 5-liter) Rocket V8 was known to be imminent. A gross power output of 160 bhp at 3800 rpm was quoted for this modern, light, oversquare, high-compression, ohv engine which – true to Cadillac tradition – consisted of eight cylinders in V configuration.

In 1950 the name of Cadillac came to be praised highly in the field of racing: chancy territory which the division eschewed under normal circumstances. This was due, entirely, to the excellent performance of the new 331 cu in (5.4-liter) engine. The venture was a private one. Sportsman Briggs Cunningham wanted to see America succeed in the 24-hour Grand Prix d'Endurance at Le Mans.

The new engine was readily available and engineer and tuner William Frick of Freeport, New York, was finding a ready market for his sports Ford conversion, the Fordillac, which Cunningham wanted to take to Le Mans in 1950. Word came back that it might not meet the regulations, so Cunningham took the prompt decision to enter two of the latest Series 61 Cadillac coupes, tuned by Frick. One was a regular "street" machine, the other was rebodied as a strange "flat-iron" open car. These unlikely vehicles completed the 24-hour event impressively, coming 10th and 11th.

Cunningham already owned a British Healey Silverstone sports car, which Frick had fitted with the new Cadillac engine in place of the original Riley unit. This was raced successfully in the United States in 1950, and helped to inspire the first of the all-American Cunningham sports-racers which ran at Le Mans between 1951 and 1955. The first Cunningham did have a Cadillac engine, but a switch was made to Chrysler when supplies dried up. Cadillac did not in fact cease supplying engines to outsiders, for Bill Frick was later able to offer his customers the superb Studillac, a combination of Studebaker's European looks (Raymond Loewy's brilliant 1953 coupe) and a tuned Cadillac V8 engine: bigger and much more powerful than Studebaker's own offerings.

Simultaneously with Cunningham, Britain's Sydney Allard was seeking more power for his famous sports cars. The Allard-Cadillac added to the fame when, partnered by Tom Cole, Allard took third place at Le Mans in 1950, the first of many successes.

ENGINE	
Type	90° V, in-line, water-cooled
No. of cylinders	8
Bore/stroke	3.8 × 3.6 in (97 × 92 mm)
Displacement	331 cu in (5440 cc)
Valve operation	Overhead
Compression ratio	8.0:1
Carburation	One four-barrel carburetor
BHP	190 gross at 4000 rpm

VEHICLE	
Transmission	Hydra-matic gearbox
Driving wheels	Rear
Length	217 in (5500 mm)
Wheelbase	130 in (3300 mm)
Weight (approx.)	4255 lb (1930 kg)
Steering	Power-assisted
Suspension – front	Independent
Suspension – rear	Rigid
Brakes	Drum

NOTES

First full year of automatic transmission standardization across the range. (Three-speed manual box virtually dropped.)

1957 Cadillac Eldorado Brougham

Cadillac Eldorado Brougham

From 1949 through 1961 (although not every year) Harley Earl orchestrated the GM extravaganza known as the Motorama, during which many a dream car became – temporarily – real. One of the best-known was Le Sabre, an exaggerated two-seater that made the old Y-job look neat, incorporating enormous tailfins plus a central "jet intake" effect front and rear. Whether it offended the eye did not matter as long as it caught it. That it surely did.

Le Sabre featured one particularly unfortunate new characteristic that was to bedevil the industry for a decade: the "panoramic" windshield. Two years after Le Sabre this idea became reality in the limited edition 1953 Eldorado Special convertible.

For 1954, the whole Cadillac range went "panoramic" mad and, over the next few years, windshield pillar bases moved further and further back, making access difficult and creating new blind spots.

Now that Cadillac "exclusivity" was being shared so widely, it was considered desirable to reestablish an expensive supercar every so often. The 500-odd 1953 Eldorado Specials had been priced close to $8000, or twice the price of a Cadillac 62 sedan.

The Eldorado theme was pursued, and reached its ultimate expression in the 1957 model year, when a new chassis frame design permitted still further lowering of the body lines. The 1957 Eldorado Brougham, which introduced the quadruple headlight arrangement, was a pillarless, four-door hardtop with innumerable built-in extras, bright color schemes and plenty of chromium plate and stainless steel. Technically it was pretty exciting, with self-adjusting compressed air suspension; this, unfortunately, was unreliable in service and left the $13,000 price tag open to criticism – for a "basic Caddy" could still be bought for less than $5000.

Since 1956, the engine size had been upped to 365 cu in (6 liters), and 325 bhp was being quoted for the Eldorado Brougham.

When Harley Earl retired at the end of the decade, the forms he had created seemed to have reached their zenith, or their nadir, depending upon your viewpoint. He had done what he had set out to do: to sell more and more Cadillacs by lowering and lengthening them. The 1959 Cadillacs had low roofs and the highest fins yet. That year's Eldorado Brougham had the painful prestige of a link with Pininfarina. The model was discontinued as an impractical proposition in 1960, for shipping to Italy and back made little sense. However, this car also started a new trend – or, rather, an about-face. The cranked-back windshield pillar was replaced by a slimmer one, angled forward. Slowly, surely, the Cadillacs of the early 1960s regained their poise, and still their market share rose.

ENGINE		VEHICLE	
Type	90° V, in-line, water-cooled	**Transmission**	Hydra-matic gearbox
No. of cylinders	8	**Driving wheels**	Rear
Bore/stroke	4 × 3.6 in (102 × 92 mm)	**Length**	217 in (5510 mm)
		Wheelbase	126 in (3200 mm)
		Weight (approx.)	5290 lb (2400 kg)
Displacement	365 cu in (5980 cc)	**Steering**	Power assistance standard
Valve operation	Overhead		
Compression ratio	10.0:1	**Suspension – front**	Independent, air
Carburation	Dual four-barrel carburetors	**Suspension – rear**	Rigid, air
		Brakes	Drum
BHP	325 gross at 4800 rpm		

NOTES

"Regular" Cadillacs had single-carburetor versions of the same engine, quoted as producing 300 bhp at 4800 rpm.

1965 Cadillac Fleetwood Eldorado

Cadillac Fleetwood Eldorado

In the 1960s, the influence of William Mitchell as Harley Earl's successor was discreet but very clear. The big car market was still strong, but the customer was no longer excited by the jetplane or even the rocket. Year by year the fins got smaller and 1965 marked their disappearance altogether, except on the "business class" Fleetwood 75 series.

Rearranged designations meant that the base models for 1965 were called Calais and the most popular middle ones De Ville. "Fleetwood" now covered the Eldorado brand name as well as the 60 Special and the vast 75 series.

The V8 engine, which had been increased to 390 cu in (6.4 liters) in 1959, underwent major revision four years later. Dimensionally it stayed the same, but it had a lighter and stronger crankshaft and cylinder block, and was an altogether sweeter-running V8 than its forerunners. From 1964 to 1967 the displacement was up to 429 cu in (7 liters) and 340 bhp at 4600 rpm was the power claimed for every Cadillac.

The 1965 personal Cadillacs were a distinct improvement from the driver's point of view, for the engine was moved 6 in (150 mm) forward without at all spoiling the weight distribution, while a redesigned subframe lowered the center of gravity still further.

From 1961 to 1966, the Eldorado name was applied only to a convertible variation of the regular range and, as such, its price was kept in the $6000 to $7000 bracket. This represented superb value for the exclusivity of a car produced at the rate of less than ten per day. Probably the similarly shelled 1964–66 De Ville convertible at $5500 was a better deal still.

Cadillac was already preparing for a new era, as environmental problems became acute in some metropolitan areas. For years there had been a small but measurable market for imported specialist cars. Although not such a direct threat to Cadillac, a new type of indigenous personal car was becoming something of a cult: this should have begun with GM's own ill-starred Chevrolet Corvair of 1960, but the idea was adapted by Ford with the sporty-looking Mustang. General Motors responded rapidly to its rival's product with its own elegant Camaro/Firebird.

Cadillac did not have a place in this category, but there was now evidence that in future a scaling down was going to take place. Not that the big American car was going to die, for there would always be a demand. "Change of emphasis" describes the scenario after 1966: the year in which Alfred Sloan, honorary chairman and grand old man of GM, passed away.

ENGINE

Type	90° V; in-line, water-cooled
No. of cylinders	8
Bore/stroke	4.1 × 4 in (105 × 102 mm)
Displacement	429 cu in (7031 cc)
Valve operation	Overhead
Compression ratio	10.5:1
Carburation	One four-barrel carburetor
BHP	340 gross at 4600 rpm

VEHICLE

Transmission	Hydra-matic three-speed gearbox
Driving wheels	Rear
Length	224 in (5680 mm)
Wheelbase	130 in (3290 mm)
Weight (approx.)	4660 lb (2115 kg)
Steering	Power assistance standard
Suspension – front	Independent
Suspension – rear	Rigid
Brakes	Drum

NOTES

New perimeter frame permitted all 1965 Cadillacs to have engine mounted 6 in (152 mm) further forward.

1967 Cadillac Eldorado Coupe

Cadillac Eldorado Coupe

Front-wheel drive was not new, but it was very new as far as the full-size American car was concerned. Exceptions had been the short-lived Cord L-29 and the stillborn Gardner and Ruxton: all victims of optimism (bred by their superb looks?) and of the Wall Street crash. Long before, early in the century, Walter Christie had made a monster that anticipated the Mini-Minor; it had front drive *and* a transverse engine. "What's new?" one might ask.

As early as 1962, Cadillac had settled for the development of a completely new front-drive car to bring the marque's drivability up to date. For 1967 the rear-wheel-drive Eldorado convertible was dropped, leaving a De Ville model for the open-air lover. It was time the Eldorado was given a character of its own. The 1967 model Eldorado Coupe was the outstanding Cadillac of the decade, and it would be made in greater quantities than previous Eldorados: 20,000 a year and more.

It is only fair to record that the Oldsmobile Toronado was announced a little earlier, taking all the kudos as the first big, modern fwd car. Built on the same foundations as the Olds, the 1967 Fleetwood Eldorado hardtop coupe was as elegant and individual as Earl's 1933 Chicago World's Fair car or Mitchell's first 60 Special: a fine exercise in clean, modern automobile sculpture.

Fwd Eldorado volumes took Cadillac production and sales past 200,000 for the first time in 1967. Another first was to exceed $2\frac{1}{2}$ percent of the new car market in the United States.

In 1968 came the introduction of a bigger engine, to compensate for necessary but power-sapping emission control devices such as air injection; 375 bhp at 4400 rpm was claimed for this mighty V8. In 1970, this unit was given a boost for the Eldorado only – 500 cu in (8.2 liters), with the nice round figure of 400 bhp in harness at the regular 4400 rpm. Up to now, the only front-wheel-drive Cadillac was the Eldorado Coupe; in 1971 Cadillac's convertible went fwd.

Figures for the 1973 model year were exceptionally good, with the 300,000 target achieved, including over 50,000 fwd models. It was in this year that casual power output claims were dropped; from now on, net bhp quotations were required. At first they looked very sad; we have gotten used to them now. Late in the year came the oil producers' embargo and Cadillac, still without a compact car, suffered accordingly. Even so, production of nearly a quarter of a million automobiles in 1974, and again in 1975, was not going to put Cadillac out of business. It had 3 percent of the home market now and, in any case, a genuine compact Cadillac was about to come into being to meet the challenge from abroad.

ENGINE		VEHICLE	
Type	90° V, in-line, water-cooled	**Transmission**	Hydra-matic three-speed gearbox
No. of cylinders	8	**Driving wheels**	Front
Bore/stroke	4.1 × 4 in (105 × 102 mm)	**Length**	221 in (5610 mm)
		Wheelbase	120 in (3050 mm)
Displacement	429 cu in (7031 cc)	**Weight (approx.)**	4850 lb (2200 kg)
Valve operation	Overhead	**Steering**	Varying ratio
Compression ratio	10.5:1	**Suspension – front**	Independent
Carburation	One four-barrel carburetor	**Suspension – rear**	Rigid
		Brakes	Drum
BHP	340 gross at 4600 rpm		

NOTES

Disk brakes at front, optional this year, would become standard shortly.

1976 Cadillac Eldorado Convertible

Cadillac Eldorado Convertible

Uniquely, Cadillac had been making V8-engined automobiles on a volume production basis for over 60 years when, in April 1975, the Seville was announced. Naturally enough, it followed tradition. Its 350 cu in (5.7-liter) power unit was from Oldsmobile and had electronic fuel injection – but it was still a V8.

Seville (not to be confused with De Ville) was something of a last resort in Cadillac's search for a new name. LaSalle and Leland had been among the worthy thoughts beforehand. Spanish-looking names were all the rage so Cadillac joined in. (The 1956–60 Eldorado hardtop had been subtitled Seville to distinguish it from the Biarritz convertible, but the tag had not been used since.)

Mid-season launches were exceptional, but this one was special. Cadillac had joined the compact campaign. The cleverness was in making the Seville a super-luxury compact, and pricing it high. After all, it was meant to make life difficult for imported supercars, as epitomized by Mercedes-Benz; and there was something in the Seville's plain, simple, but very carefully designed appearance that made it look more European than American from certain angles. If Rolls-Royce had copied the 1948 sedanet for its Bentley Continental, surely no one would take exception now to a hint from that quarter for the new Cadillac.

Speed of development, because of the 1973 oil crisis, meant that the Seville was introduced as a car of mechanical orthodoxy. Despite this, and a price that inflated from $12,000 to $16,000, production of the new-look Cadillac averaged over 50,000 units annually during its four-year run to 1979.

It did not take long for the Seville style to influence that of the bigger Cadillacs, which began to shrink. Front-wheel drive was still confined to the Eldorado (no longer as lithe-looking as it had been), the convertible version of which was discontinued after 1976. At the time this was declared, even by Cadillac, to be the last of the breed: but subsequent events have proved that the open car still has a lively future.

The Calais series disappeared in 1976 and the 1977 Coupe de Ville was the last Cadillac to be listed at under $10,000. With over 3 percent of an increasingly buoyant market, price was no more a problem to Cadillac than ever it had been.

Meeting the Federal laws and retaining the customer's affections were all-important. The De Ville remained a great favorite as the all-purpose symbol of workaday wealth. In 1977 there was a reduction of engine size from 500 to 425 cu in (8.2 to 7 liters); and there were to be many more changes in the range for the 1980s.

ENGINE		VEHICLE	
Type	90° V, in-line, water-cooled	**Transmission**	Hydra-matic three-speed gearbox
No. of cylinders	8	**Driving wheels**	Front
Bore/stroke	4.3 × 4.3 in (109 × 109 mm)	**Length**	224 in (5690 mm)
Displacement	500 cu in (8194 cc)	**Wheelbase**	126 in (3210 mm)
Valve operation	Overhead	**Weight (approx.)**	5290 lb (2400 kg)
Compression ratio	8.5:1	**Steering**	Varying ratio
Carburation	One four-barrel carburetor	**Suspension – front**	Independent
BHP	190 at 3600 rpm	**Suspension – rear**	Rigid
		Brakes	Disk all round

NOTES

215 bhp EFI version also offered. (Final year of 8.2-liter engine.)

1980 Cadillac Seville Elegante

Cadillac Seville Elegante

The new Cadillac of 1979 was the compact Eldorado. The squared-off tail of the 1976 Seville had, perhaps, inspired the way in which it was done, for the latest Eldorado's lines were almost severe. Wheelbase was reduced by more than 12 in (305 mm). The Eldorado kept its front-wheel drive, naturally, but had the smaller (Seville) 350 cu in (5.7-liter) V8 engine, which was quite economical. In September 1979, a completely new Seville was announced, with the wheelbase and general layout of the latest Eldorado. It had disk brakes and independent suspension all round, and front-wheel drive – as had been the original intention. As with the Eldorado, there was a choice between the regular gasoline engine and a diesel version of it. The 1980 Seville was dramatic to look at. The recent tendency had been to give Cadillacs a near-vertical rear window. Now this had been sharply raked and the rest of the bodywork altered to suit. The effect was a series of curves sweeping down to merge at rear bumper level. Hooper of London had created the style in the late 1940s; Jaguar's Daimler limousine has been featuring it since 1968. William Mitchell and his team were brave to revive the idea for 1980, and the distinctive Seville rewarded Cadillac with considerable publicity. It was announced as the first car ever to be sold with diesel engine, front-wheel drive, all-disk braking, cruise control, electronic climate control, and all-independent suspension with electronic leveling as standard.

Although it looked unique, the 1980–85 Seville was in fact built on the same base as the Buick Riviera, the Oldsmobile Toronado and, of course, its colleague the Eldorado at GM's New Jersey factory. From some angles, and in the right light, that particular Cadillac could look stunning. For 1986, however, the Seville and the Eldorado would change drastically yet again.

The need to be fuel efficient resulted in numerous changes in the early 1980s, when sales fell again. There was the notorious V8-6-4 gasoline engine in which an electronic system was meant to cut out the operation of unnecessary cylinders, but this never worked smoothly. More of a success was Buick's 250 cu in (4.1-liter) V6, used briefly until Cadillac's own new 250 cu in V8 was ready.

Frantic for sales, Cadillac even put its name to the GM J-car (in fact a Vauxhall Cavalier) and called it the 1982 Cimarron. There had not been a four-cylinder Cadillac since 1914. And there was little about it to which the traditional Cadillac buyer could relate.

In 1984 there was light relief in the knowledge that the convertible Eldorado was back, and it was much smaller than its predecessors. A Cadillac sports car? Well – not quite.

ENGINE		VEHICLE	
Type	90° V, in-line, water-cooled	**Transmission**	Four-speed automatic gearbox, with overdrive
No. of cylinders	8 *(see Notes)*	**Driving wheels**	Front
Bore/stroke	4 × 3.4 in (103 × 86 mm)	**Length**	206 in (5220 mm)
Displacement	350 cu in (5737 cc)	**Wheelbase**	114 in (2895 mm)
Valve operation	Overhead	**Weight (approx.)**	3810 lb (1730 kg)
Compression ratio	8.0:1	**Steering**	Recirculating ball
Carburation	Electronic fuel injection	**Suspension – front**	Independent
		Suspension – rear	Independent
BHP	180 at 4400 rpm	**Brakes**	Disk all round

NOTES

Diesel versions of the 5.7-liter engine (plus 6-liter V8, 4.1-liter V6, and 4.1 liter V8 gasoline units) were also used for "second generation" Sevilles.

1986 Cadillac Seville

Cadillac Seville

Since 1941 there has been a Cadillac series called the Fleetwood 75. Up to 1984 it retained its traditional layout: front engine and rear-wheel drive. For 1985 it underwent its greatest change ever, adopting front-wheel drive and all-independent suspension, as did the De Ville. The engines of these new models were mounted transversely in order to use the space better.

In 1985 there remained a pair of classic Cadillacs. The Fleetwood Brougham Sedan and Coupe were still in production. Everything else had followed the front-drive path. All models except the Cimarron were fitted with Cadillac's own digital fuel-injection 250 cu in (4.1-liter) V8 as standard, but there were advantages for some. For no extra charge, an Oldsmobile 260 cu in (4.3-liter) V6 diesel could be ordered for the new front-wheel drive De Ville and owner-driver Fleetwood (but not the 75). Another Oldsmobile diesel, the 350 cu in (5.7-liter) V8, could be specified for certain Eldorados, the rear-wheel-drive Fleetwood Brougham and the Seville. All these models now had a four-speed automatic transmission with overdrive.

The little Cimarron could be offered with a 170 cu in (2.8-liter) V6 as an extra-cost alternative to the 120 cu in (2-liter) four.

There were further sweeping changes for 1986. Cadillac's prestige personal cars, the Eldorado two-door and the Seville four-door, became true compacts. They were fully 16 in (406 mm) shorter than their immediate predecessors. They retained the DFI 250 cu in (4.1-liter) V8 as standard, but it was now placed crosswise. A four-speed automatic transmission unit with overdrive was still fitted, plus a viscous converter clutch.

By 1986 only one ''traditional'' Cadillac was still being listed: the Fleetwood Brougham in its basic and ''Sedan d'Elégance'' forms. This 305 cu in (5-liter) V8-powered rear-drive luxury car was probably not the last of the line, despite the fact that front drive and transverse engine mounting typified the rest of the Cadillac range: GM has stated its intentions to continue with rear-wheel-drive models as long as a market for them remains. For decades, the US industry has been compromising on compact cars. With the 1986 Eldorados and Sevilles, and the new Allanté for 1987, GM's Cadillac division appeared to grasp the nettle.

Cadillac can be seen to be moving with the times: maintaining its reputation and profitability on behalf of General Motors, the world's largest automobile corporation.

ENGINE		VEHICLE	
Type	90° V, transverse, water-cooled	**Transmission**	Four-speed automatic gearbox, with overdrive
No. of cylinders	8	**Driving wheels**	Front
Bore/stroke	3.5 × 1.7 in (88 × 44 mm)	**Length**	188 in (4780 mm)
Displacement	250 cu in (4087 cc)	**Wheelbase**	108 in (2743 mm)
Valve operation	Overhead	**Weight (approx.)**	3428 lb (1555 kg)
Compression ratio	8.5:1	**Steering**	Rack & pinion
Carburation	Digital fuel injection	**Suspension – front**	Independent
BHP	130 at 4200 rpm	**Suspension – rear**	Independent
		Brakes	Disk all round

NOTES

1986 Eldorado 2-door range had similar mechanical specification, and weighed slightly less.